Cracked Open

poems by

Thayer Cory

Finishing Line Press
Georgetown, Kentucky

Cracked Open

*For Tom,
my best listener and cheerleader*

Copyright © 2018 by Thayer Cory
ISBN 978-1-63534-420-2 First Edition
All rights reserved under International and Pan-American Copyright Conventions. No part of this book may be reproduced in any manner whatsoever without written permission from the publisher, except in the case of brief quotations embodied in critical articles and reviews.

ACKNOWLEDGMENTS

With deep gratitude to Mary De Lara and all the members of The Williamsburg Poetry Guild for their generous support, trust and feedback. Thanks to Joanne Goode who tosses me ideas and keeps me writing and singing. And special thanks to Phyllis Haislip who encouraged me to begin this project, then held my hand while I completed it.

Publisher: Leah Maines
Editor: Christen Kincaid
Cover Art: Thayer Cory
Author Photo: John Goode
Cover Design: Elizabeth Maines McCleavy

Printed in the USA on acid-free paper.
Order online: www.finishinglinepress.com
also available on amazon.com

Author inquiries and mail orders:
Finishing Line Press
P. O. Box 1626
Georgetown, Kentucky 40324
U. S. A.

Table of Contents

Epiphany 1
Planting Onions 2
Daffodils in Snow 3
Amagansett: End of Summer 4
Montana Hymn 5
Cracked Open 6
Monastere des Filles de Jesus 7
Elegy for Suzanne 8
The Wound 9
Visitor 10
These Boys 11
Initiation 12
After 14
Mornings 15
Sitting In Silence without You 16
After 64 Years 17
This Still House 19
The Thread of Time 20
Freckles 21
Subway 22
Opening 24
Summer 1968 26
Sleep 28
Rosie 30
All I Want for Christmas 31
Amagansett 33

Epiphany

It was two goats
statue still
behind the fence
eyes gray
glassy as marbles

It was the tufts
of grass
they stood on
the clumsy sheep
behind them
and the clods of earth
all dark and damp

It was the way
as we drew near
they inched
stupidly towards Tom
and the way
he scratched their noses

That sent the shards
of the kaleidoscope
tumbling turning everything
suddenly precious

It was then I knew
that somewhere deep inside
goats sing praises
sheep rejoice
grass adores its loveliness
and dirt is lit from within

Planting Onions

She is no farmer
but she bends
to the earth, knows
its emptiness,
its longing. She has
come to the farm
to plant onions, small
tasseled pearls to be sown
in small wounds—
red, white and yellow
bulbs made snug
in hopeful soil.

She muses on the row
that's been given her,
measures four inches
between plantings.
An old anxiety
about doing it perfectly
argues with the knowledge
that earth is forgiving.

She doubts her place in this world
and lacks the peace of simple things.
But for now her mind is bent
to the darkness before her,
to the dirt that feeds the onions,
that coaxes them dumbly
to take root, to grow.

Daffodils in Snow

They open their purses
        and cold coins pour in

Star faces bow
        sheltering backs bend

The long earth sleep
        has ended too soon

Winter's icy shadow stalks
        all that is waking

Still green ladders ascend
        trusting the sun

The brown knowledge
        of dirt of themselves

They stretch to heaven
        heedless of the white dark

Amagansett: End of Summer

There's relief in the air.
The beach breathes easy,
the breeze no longer perfumed
by the oiled scent of summer people.

The ocean sighs,
yields to a lone swimmer
who is lifted and tossed,
his red shorts a single drop
of blood in cold, gray waves.

At the farmer's stand
fiery tomatoes rush into ripeness,
fans of chard lie dark and hopeful.
The edge of our road brightens
with yellowing fronds of goldenrod
and leaves, their purpose served,
begin to relax.

On Main Street, end-of-summer sales
pull us into quiet shops, push us
out with bags of bargains.
It's possible to cross the street now,
to dream a little on a village bench.

The tasks of continuing call me
but I am reluctant to listen,
content for a moment to let
absence hallow the air.
Its presence sweeps the beach.
Its empty arms promise nothing.

Montana Hymn
    for Susan

Praise for the wheel of sun
rolling across the morning sky,
the swallow cartwheeling in air
before diving into her tree-house home.

Praise for distant mountains
mantled in snow,
tall grasses flashing in the pasture
during the long song of this day.

Praise for wildflowers—chorus of pink,
purple, yellow, layers of white—
in perfect harmony
rising to rejoice.

Praise for the silver stream
that sings without ceasing,
cows and calves anointed by light
amid clouds come to cool the afternoon.

Praise for the cottonwood choir
whispering the house to sleep,
the glow of mountain embers
finally fading into ash.

Praise for the falling dark.

Cracked Open
> *There is a crack in everything. That is how the light gets in.*
> Leonard Cohen

On an October evening
as my body sags
from carrying grandbabies,
a frightened daughter,
her father my former husband
who languishes alone
in a Norfolk hospital bed,
and my brain spins
with scenarios that all end badly,
a friend brings dinner.
Not just a casserole—a casserole
and green beans, biscuits, brownies.
*Those of us who weren't mothered
properly,* she says, *must learn to
mother each other.* She returns
the next night with chicken,
roasted roots and salad.

I stand in my doorway,
empty, and receive
the nourishment I need.
If I hadn't been
so tired and cracked open
I wouldn't be accepting
this bounty. Suddenly
it seems possible
that every vulnerability can be
an opening that lets
healing touch us,
every need a chance for light
to break through.

Monastere des Filles de Jesus—On the Camino de Santiago

Stooped by our packs,
wilted by the heat of noon,
we came seeking refuge,
a pilgrim's need.
We must have looked like beggars
as we stood outside the door
waiting to be received
into this fellowship of loss,
a home for the old and hunched,
the withered roots come
to rest after laboring
in the fields of the Lord.
The nun who welcomed us
searched my eyes, my soul.
I fear her plumb line came up short.
They fed us and let us hang
our laundry on backyard lines.
Later, we listened to their
chants, tremulous sopranos
in perfect pitch.
Wizened whispers ascended
the vaulted ceiling of their chapel,
dropped into my weary frame.
There were morning stars
when we woke. We departed
and walked the way lightly,
carried, as we were,
on the bent back of God.

Elegy for Suzanne

The peonies, their pale pink fists still taut,
will burst and flare again though you are gone,
then bend to time's worn hand just as they ought—
The mystery of bloom and death is one.
You loved your life but fought with death, enraged
by early loss, an orphaned child's plight.
With fierce and pointed will you turned, then faced
the equal measures brought by dark and light.
When cancer came, your heart, encased in grief
for all the joys you'd lose, was filled with fear.
We prayed for grace—acceptance of the thief
who robs us—and brings peonies each year.
The mystery runs deep in lessons taught—
To wake, to bloom, to die just as we ought.

The Wound

I galloped through the house that summer morning, calling, "Ruthie, Ruthie," until I found you coming down the stairs, basket of laundry in your arms. "We're going to the beach." I was breathless. "Come on!" "Get ready!" You gripped the sides of the basket and gazed at me, your dark eyes searching. "I can't go to that beach," you said flatly. My heart lurched. Something sharp pierced my chest. I already knew why you couldn't go to that beach. The answer, bone deep for most of my five years, weighed me down, made me ache. Your skin was the color of creamed coffee; mine was fair and freckled. There were other differences—shadows I couldn't name, sorrow that pursued you like a hungry dog. Protest rose in my throat, tingled down my arms. I could only gape. After a long moment, you adjusted the basket and continued down the stairs. Mother called and I went to the beach. I tasted the wound in picnic sandwiches, heard its cry in the hissing waves. Its salt-smell stung my nostrils. It clung like wet sand to my thin limbs. Then it receded into the back room of my heart where it would bleed into everything I did. Into everything I became.

Visitor

One night, in the Japanese darkness,
as loneliness stripped me
and wrung blind tears from
my unformed, teenaged heart,

I woke to find a bat inches from my nose.
No screen on the window, just bat
settling on the sill, staring
at my pulsing throat.

In the morning my host family
laughed, said they'd never
seen such a thing.

The bat did not return,

but for the rest of the summer
I waited—watching
in this foreign land
as terror, relief,
something like happiness
flew through the window,
entered my body,
found my pulse.

These Boys

They hurl themselves
at the ocean's jaw—
three backs glistening,
muscles bronzed with sun,
hair wet as when they were born.

Coughed up on the beach,
they rise triumphant,
race back to ride the snarling lip.
Foam-flecked teeth gnash
their small, quick bodies,
try to grind them
into sea-glass smoothness.

They are in their element—
fish-flesh children,
immersed and wide-eyed,
seeing nothing. They roll
in happiness, baptized
again and again
by the relentless sea.

And I, shore-planted,
wrapped in beach chair
and sunglasses, am tossed
between fear and admiration
for these boys and for the blind
indifference carrying them,
for now, to victory.

Initiation

We waited on the platform
that birthday morning.
We had already opened presents—
two piles, equally numbered
to minimize the competition of twins.
I don't remember what we got.
It didn't matter.
Sitting on the scratchy summer rug,
everyone watching,
being at the center; that mattered.
We wore identical clothes—khaki shorts,
blue-and-white gingham shirts, red sneakers.
I liked that—even if you were a boy.
Breakfast over and there we were
at the Amagansett train station.
We had stood there many times before.
Eager, jumpy with excitement,
we'd put pennies on the track,
run skittering to safety,
strain to hear the whistle,
close our eyes and feel the rush of
wind that stole our breath
as the train sped in.
Our father was the prize,
deposited on the platform
weary and smiling as the train
groaned and slipped away.
But on that morning
he was with us, pacing in anticipation,
relishing the wait, talking train lore,
excited as a boy.
Then, the behemoth stood
beside us, still, inviting.
The engineer stepped down and shook your hand
as if you were a grown-up.

I watched as you followed him
up the steps and disappeared into the cabin.
You reappeared at the window
with an engineer's cap and a grin.
Your thick glasses hid your eyes
but not your delight.
I complained. "It isn't fair."
Mother said to wave and smile
and be glad for you—
for such a splendid birthday gift.
The engine hissed and inched away.
Like a wind-up doll glued to the concrete
I waved and smiled, waved and smiled
as the train moved on.
And you and Dad and the engineer,
three charioteers, three warriors off to battle,
three hunters eager for the kill,
rode twelve glorious miles—
all the way to Montauk Point.

After

After my brother got into a row boat and flung
our mother's ashes into Gardiner's Bay,
we came back to the house and drank wine,
told stories, tried to remember who she had been,
where we had come from. But she slipped
away as she always did. Before long
the grandchildren were restless
and we were laughing at old jokes,
settling into a comfort that we'd woven
without her—the thread of her absence
pulling the five of us tighter, like a drawstring
tugging the fabric of our history into folds
so we could touch each other, be close enough
to find the familiar strangers we'd grown up with.

Mornings

      Morning after morning we wake, turn,
your tall frame curling around my back.
      We hold each other, two commas pausing,
breath dissolving in the early darkness.

      No words, perhaps a happy purr,
silence wrapping us in a delicate web,
      keeping the warring world at bay.
We are not young or old, male or female, flesh or stone

      Only the essence of perfection held
beneath the covers, a private union
      complete as a prayer, a moment of grace
before daylight brings us back into ourselves.

Sitting in Silence without You

Old woman, almost seventy-five now,
still hunched on your yoga pillow
attempting to melt past and future
in the furnace of now, I see you
and smile. You will never give up.

We will sit here in silence all morning—
our monthly ritual punctuated
by a walk on the beach and lunch
concocted by you; spicy soup
and fragrant cheese, homemade bread,
perhaps some sorbet.

We will embrace our hunger
for boundaries, the reaches
of spirit, the delicious, terrifying
mystery. Abundance is our calling
and with long, slow attention
we will watch it rise up, brim over.

I smile with joy seeing you now,
almost eleven years after your death.
The silence between us has turned
and turned, has sunk down to its seed
and rests comfortably deep within.

Here it is late afternoon.
Snow comes down in heavy veils.
I stand in my kitchen watching you
in silence, accompanied by good smells
and dancing pot lids.

After 64 Years
for Jolen on her 70th birthday

Beneath the surface, under the freckles
and lines, curves and ridges
that look like a topographic map,
the girl you were is still growing,
still skinning her knees with tomboy intensity,
still lifting the scabs to peek into the future.

You were known by your dogs. Always the dogs.
I laugh out loud when I think of you
rolling on the floor with Dandy or Cocoa—
poodle partners in vulnerability,
harbors in the treacherous seas of home.
Even now you march into a café,
scold the owner of a shivering dog left outside
for not providing a coat.

What generous attention.
See how it turns to include us, your friends,
the ones you pursue when we've gone astray,
the ones you rope in, reminding us that loyalty is forever.

And your powers of reinvention.
Do you remember how you refused
to mince across the stage as a sister or cousin or aunt
in Mrs. Miller's fourth grade production of HMS Pinafore,
how you persuaded her to let us vote
so you could be a sailor instead? You still refuse
to be molded into what doesn't fit you.

How many times have you pulled yourself up,
come back from some flattening, determination rising
like a geyser, spilling you hot into
new places, shapes, skills you didn't know you had.

Dear friend, you still have gravel in your knees
and it makes you tough as a stained buffalo hide
and tender as an old dog's belly.
You grow old. But you grow,
with unflinching courage and love lapping at your heels.

This Still House

Gray light of morning
presses through the window.
You and the dog remain
lost in sleep. I try to read you,
silent under the covers,
but there is nothing new—
only the constant
making my heart shiver,
the worry skittering
across my mind,
a dawning—a thousand times
new—that the light is shifting,
there is no safe passage,
only that I must rise
into what life I have left
and walk jubilantly
into our wounded world
in spite of what I know.

The Thread of Time—A Villanelle
for A.P.

The trailing thread of time can strangle dreams
by twisting innate hopes, sweet love's desires.
The present is not always what it seems.

Memories form writhing eels that teem
and flail in brains so young hard-wired.
The trailing thread of time will strangle dreams.

Cruelty, losses, lacks will reign supreme,
electrocute the impulse to aspire.
The present is not always what it seems.

Repeat the lines, swim round or jump upstream—
in tight-roped nets we squirm until we tire.
The trailing thread of time can strangle dreams.

To swim we must unravel all those streams,
find heart; see new; the tattered old retire.
The present is not always what it seems.

Our spirits rise, push through dark-water screens,
demand the light—it's what a life requires.
The thread of time can't strangle all our dreams.
The present can be sometimes what it seems.

Freckles

Every sunny summer
a crop of freckles
bloomed across my nose,
my cheeks.

Splashy browns
staining my face,
bronze stars
glowing on pink sky.

Cuteness on one still young,
badges of despair
to a self-conscious teen,
dreaded at age forty-five.

After so many winters
they've run together,
relaxing, drifting
into pools and lines.

I search the mirror,
try to read
their scribbled story.
They speak of what I've lost.

Now my face wears
what I've earned—
valleys and ridges,
dips and curves
mapped by me—
a starry, wrinkled flag
I raise and feel content.

Subway

inside the L train at 7:45 am   the faithful
burrow into their   skins   stop ears with
musical buttons   gaze into the middle
distance   or   read

doors gasp open   wide mouths   spit out some
suck in others   close with a sigh   bullet
hurtles down dusky tunnel   screaming
startingstopping   syncopated wheels   rock
passengers   who appear unmoved

hands close on poles   or overhead handles
knees and thighs   escape touch   by fractions
of inches   in intimate indifference   with
measured politeness   new york pilgrims
head to   secret   destinations

the schizophrenic   and his dusty dog
careen   through the car   but only the woman
in red tights   and black jacket is roused
puts change in   his bag

the white man   in natty suit   helps
the grizzled   black   man   decipher the map
tells him   where to change trains
the   student   and   his cello   hog   two   seats

the angelic hipster   with nose   ring
and hole in his   ear   the size of a nickel
rises from his reverie   unfolds from his seat
nods his wired head   to the old woman
who shuffles over   takes   his place

every day   the faithful enter   the silver cocoon
huddle with strangers   cradle
their stories calculate   theirspace   closeness
distance   awake   asleep   they trust
they   will be   delivered

Opening

A plodding, patient housefly
walks a ragged route along the glass,
feels a phantom edge, turns
and like a swimmer
completes a perfect lap.
Up and back, up and back,
he misses nothing in his path,
this black-winged marching soldier,
this prisoner pacing in his cell.

Suddenly, all patience lost,
he hurls himself
into the window pane.
The buzz and hiss
of helpless fury fill the porch.
He stops. Returns
to find his place,
resume his lonely trek.
Up and back, up and back.

Oh plodding housefly!
What blindness keeps you
from the freedom
that you crave
while just two feet away
the door yawns open?

And you, my soul?
How you cling
in mute refusal,
caught in patterns,
measuring endless ruts,
longing for a door to yield
so you can join the stars and sun.
Could it be
that if you dared to lift your head—
a mere shift of shadows—
you would see the light?

Summer 1968

Martin Luther King dead in April.
Bobby Kennedy gone in June.
I'd come to Roanoke, a naïve northerner,
not quite 21, fired to walk the injustice walk,
take on racism, raise my fist in outrage.
Secretly I longed for adventure, a chance
to break away from my Boston box.

From New York and Massachusetts,
Washington, D.C. and New Jersey,
we came; well-meaning white students,
housed in a church basement,
ready to work in a local day camp,
teach poor black kids how to swim.

I'd never seen a gun up close.
I saw them now—in jacket pockets
and glove compartments,
hidden in living room drawers.
The local program coordinator
carried a sweet piece with a pink handle.

Folks from the housing project befriended us—
boys who went to Norfolk State,
girls who eyed us warily,
mothers who welcomed us into their homes,
fed us fried chicken.

I don't remember who hatched the plan.
We would go, a mixed-race group,
to the local amusement park.
The black boys were tense, poised for action.
They knew this territory. The black girls
held back, afraid. We whites were excited,
eager to be part of something big.

Nigger lover. The words were hissed.
They hit like stinging sand. *White trash!*
Go home. My stomach clenched,
bones in my legs dissolved.
I willed my head high and walked on.

A group of local white boys followed us,
taunting. The slurs got meaner, dirtier.
Someone in our group said, *Let's go* and we bolted
for the parking lot. The townies followed,
jumped into their pickup, rifle strapped
across the back window. *Lie on the floor!*
our driver ordered as he pulled out his gun.

They tailgated, pulled in front,
tried to run us off the road. They sneered
and shouted names. We lost them
when we turned into the project.
They knew enough not to go there.
I stumbled from the car, lurched into the house.
The mother of a Norfolk State boy took one look at me,
said, *Honey, you sit down.* I began to shake, to sob.
What exactly would justice require?

Sleep

Sleep drapes her silky self across the chair in the corner.
She is filing her nails, paying no attention to me.

I want to entice her to lay her soft sheets,
full of kindness and healing, over my weary body.

Even though I'm bone tired, I can tell she's not ready.
She's like that. I try not to be annoyed.

Look, I say, *I can take ten deep breaths,
counting four breathing in, eight breathing out.*

She is unimpressed but flings me a look with hooded eyes.
At least that. She's noticed that I'm calling her.

I'm sorry, I plead. *I didn't want to have that negative thought.
They sometimes come unbidden even when I push them away.*

She doesn't like negative thoughts and won't be seen with them.
I beg her to ignore them, but always honest, she will not comply.

I try another trick. *See? I can go to my happy place.
Watch me lying in the sun, sooo relaxed. You like that, right?*

She does. Like a cautious cat, she rises, stretches, inches
forward, then stops to gaze out the window at the waxing moon.

In irritation, I tell her I might try a sleeping pill. Her eyes pivot.
She likes a crumb of Ambien and will always come for that.

But Ambien scares me and reminds me of my failure.
I roll over, wide-awake. Will she ever be satisfied?

She blows on her nails, stretches her fingers, gives me
a kind look. I feel its warmth on my back. Still, she refuses.

Then, when I've resigned myself to a night without her, she lays
her gentle hands on my chest, her mantle across my shoulders.

Rosie

It defies reason how we dote on Rosie,
our rescued border collie/ Brittany spaniel mix.
Bronze and snow, bounding bundle of tongue and tail,
she jumps on our bed, nuzzles between us,
turns on her back and pretends to read the air
while we read our books and magazines.
She would lick off our faces if we let her, but is content
to bathe our paws, which she does with careful concentration.
She whimpers when a grandchild cries, wants to kiss
and comfort, tell us how it should be done.
In our neighbor's yard she flings herself
at her pals, Buddy and Bingo— unfettered spirit
in glorious freedom, creature of the wild.
What unruly part of our souls does she unleash?
What door in our hearts does she bang open,
romp right into? When Rosie rests in her special chair,
chin on the armrest, dark eyes tracking our moves
or body dropped in stone-deep sleep, our tongues gush
tenderness, our tails wag in simple joy.

All I Want for Christmas

There will be no quiet—
   talking toddlers,
      patter of small feet inescapable,
         baby bodies swooped away
            from treacherous stairs,
               howling protests, laughter.

The kitchen will overflow, meal after meal—
   gluten-free, vegetarian, who won't eat onions
      and who's allergic to tomatoes but insists
         on meat? The frig will be stuffed, I'll search
            for the lemon bought for a purpose, the
               butter that's not in its normal place.
                  The babies will nap. Please!

There will be wrapping paper
   spilling onto the dining room table,
      the scotch tape will disappear, who took
         the scissors? Presents in all corners
            and don't forget the stockings, each
               child's name embroidered on top by
                  the good folks at Land's End.

There will be tension when the dog barks
   for too long, the babies get too tired
      and sleep-deprived grown-ups unravel,
         head for the wine. There will be quick
            conversations caught while peeling carrots,
               clicking stroller straps, wiping faces.

    Music will fill the house.
        Christmas carols, guitars
            for good-night songs. Someone
                will put on jazz, someone else
                    will find John McCutcheon.
                        I'll insist on Handel's Messiah,
                            will rock a toddler and listen.

All I want for Christmas is noise, tension,
    a crowded kitchen, chronic messes, sticky children,
        truncated conversations. This music. Only this.

Amagansett
> *Have you a place where, when the world ends, you want to be?*
> *William Stafford*

Here where the sea
    breathes in and out
        a steady pulse of always

Where sand-stunted pines
    and snarled underbrush
        link arms around the house

Here between the scalloped hem
    of the tide line
        and the smooth rim of the world

Where waves unfurl their ruin
    and primal shell homes
        whisper *Listen Now*

I will be here where the dog chases
    sandpipers up the beach
        and the buoyant moon swims into the night

Where water's colors rinse
    the dune and even clouds
        have useful things to say

Here we gather around the worn table
    eat bluefish and peaches
        pour stories from cup to broken cup

It's here that dusk bends over me
    reveals a voice within my voice
        a shadow deeper than my own

Here a prayer
    from long ago
        chants *world without end Amen Amen*

Thayer Cory was raised with four siblings in New Jersey, but feels most at home on the shore of eastern Long Island and in the wilds of New England. After college (political science) and graduate school (psychology and religion) in the Boston area, she moved to Williamsburg, Virginia where she raised two children and helped raise two stepchildren. She and her husband are avid hikers and have walked through much of Europe including the Camino de Santiago in France and Spain. Her work as a psychotherapist in both public and private settings for thirty-five years continually inspires her to see the world from many perspectives, and her involvement in Williamsburg Friends Meeting (Quakers) keeps her grounded in a spiritual community. Her commitment to her four children and eight grandchildren is also a driving force in her life. All these experiences nurture and inform her poetry. Her poems search for the threads that keep us connected to human relationships, to the natural world and to the divine.

CPSIA information can be obtained
at www.ICGtesting.com
Printed in the USA
LVOW10s0605260218
567856LV00001BA/42/P

9 781635 344202